The Decompression Workbook

A simplified guide to understanding decompression problems

by George S. Lewbel, Ph.D.

 Pisces Books

New York, NY

ISBN: 0-86636-023-9

Cover photograph by George E. Lewbel

10 9 8 7 6 5 4 3 2 1

ACKNOWLEDGMENTS

The author is grateful to Commander James B. Williams (USN ret.); to Larry R. Martin, a colleague at LGL Ecological Research Associates, Inc., who is responsible for most of the Word to the Wise (p. 11); to James R. Stewart of the Scripps Institution of Oceanography; to Gregory S. Boland, also of LGL; and to Nancy R. Hofmann, Herb Taylor, and Sally Sutherland for encouragement and assistance.

CONTENTS

PREFACE

This book was written for two reasons. First, it is designed to be a teaching aid for scuba classes. Teaching decompression usually takes a lot of classroom time. If you're an instructor, you can shorten this time greatly by having your students prepare for class by doing assigned problems from this book. If you're a student, you will understand the course material far better when you use this book along with your dive manual. Second, this book will provide "rusty" sport divers with a comprehensive review of decompression procedures. If it's been a few months since your scuba course or your last dive, you may be surprised at how much you've forgotten about the tables—especially if you were a bit shaky on them the first time around! A few decompression problems on a certification exam may not do you much good when you're sitting on a boat six months later.

Even if you use one of the new automatic dive computers, you'll want to be fully proficient with the decompression tables. Most dive computers or timers are based on the U.S. Navy tables (usually with some safety factor added). No matter how well built it may be, any device can fail, whether through damage, dead battery, etc. Given the cost of a day of diving, or possible treatment in a recompression chamber, can you afford not to carry—and be competent with— a set of the tables?

FOREWORD

Historically, few students have come away from basic sport diving certification classes with more than a cursory understanding of the decompression tables. This book should go a long way toward improving the situation—which definitely needs to be improved.

For instance, the Catalina Marine Science Center (a major recompression treatment and research facility) has treated nearly 375 cases of decompression sickness and air embolism in the past nine years. I asked Dr. Andrew Pilmanis, the Associate Director, what he felt were the most common causes of bends. During the first few years, he noted, about a third of the cases were associated with the rather primitive decompression meters then available. Now, however, injured divers most frequently report that they did not have depth gauges and watches along on dives, or that they did not pay attention to this equipment; that they had never learned to use the tables properly, or that they hadn't used them since their basic class and may have been too embarrassed to ask for help. Many victims thought that depth gauges were accurate forever. Some said that their diving instructors hadn't really stressed the consequences of decompression sickness. Still others had "stretched" the tables before with no problems, and thus thought that they were somehow different from other divers in vulnerability. In other words, *diver error* is the major factor these days in decompression sickness in sport diving.

An initial understanding of the theory and concepts of decompression and the practical day-to-day use of the decompression tables can significantly reduce the chances of making these (sometimes fatal) errors. It is by no means inevitable that divers eventually get the bends. For proof, consider the Scripps Institution of Oceanography research diving program, the oldest in the United States. During its 32 years of existence, Scripps divers (using U.S. Navy Decompression Tables) have logged nearly 180,000 dives. There has only been one case of decompression sickness among these divers, and that dive fell within the U.S. Navy no-decompression limits.

These statistics make the point that there are a lot of sport divers who can benefit by a workbook such as this. Through its varied problem sets and concepts, divers at all levels can obtain a clearly written and concise overview of the practical use of the decompression tables and their application to safe dive planning and practices.

— James R. Stewart
Diving Officer
Scripps Institution
of Oceanography
December, 1983

INTRODUCTION: How to Use This Book

This workbook is not intended as a diving manual or a replacement for proper diving instruction, but, rather, as a learning supplement to any basic or advanced sport diving course taught by a qualified diving instructor, or as a review for certified sport divers who need practice with decompression problems. It is based on the U.S. Navy Diving Manual's Air Decompression tables, with supplementary material from the U.S. National Oceanic and Atmospheric Administration Diving Manual. Questions and problems emphasize no-decompression diving, and are pertinent only to scuba diving with compressed air on dives that begin and end at sea level.

The self-teaching text is divided into four sections, each containing a number of sets of 5 problems. Section 1 presents definitions and simple, one-dive problems. Section 2 introduces repetitive dives and two-dive problems. Section 3 includes problems with three and four dives in a row. Section 4 covers "errors," e.g., omitted decompression, accidental overstays, fast ascents, etc., and such topics as flying after diving. Solved examples with complete explanations are given for each problem set. For most problem sets, there are a few questions about definitions, principles, and procedures for working the tables correctly. The Appendix deals with shallow dives.

You should use your own tables—preferably, those you take with you on dive trips—for the problems, since various configurations are common. Any set of tables derived from the U.S. Navy Air Decompression tables will be fine. If you can't answer the questions right away, first try to work through the examples and explanations, do the problems, and then return to the questions. Don't start a new problem set until you understand all of the questions and problems in the previous set. If you get baffled, there is an answer key at the end of the book. You should refer to your diving manual or ask your instructor if you don't get them all right or don't understand why an answer is correct. By the time you have completed the book, you will know how to work virtually any decompression problem you're ever likely to encounter.

READ THIS: A Word to the Wise

Most good sport divers consider themselves capable and knowledgeable, and never expect to have to see the inside of a recompression chamber. They are engaged in a leisure activity to have fun. This alone should affect their dive profiles, and ideally, should be a factor in reducing their exposure to the bends. Does it work that way? Unfortunately, it often doesn't. In fact, all too frequently, sport divers subject themselves to unnecessarily high risks of decompression sickness through table misuse or sloppy diving techniques. We will cover some of the more obvious blunders in Section 4, such as inadvertently exceeding planned maximum depths and bottom times, or slow or rapid ascents. Other risks aren't always quite so apparent. For example, there is a correct procedure for calculating decompression schedules for exceptionally cold or strenuous dives. On every sport dive, there are at least two buddies. What if one of them is out of shape, or has a wetsuit that's ready for the Smithsonian? A routine dive for one buddy may be a freezing, arduous dive for the other.

The procedures mastered using this manual are the "correct" way the U.S. Navy tables were designed and intended to be used by military divers. Most sport divers who rely on the schedules given in these tables also try to use the same procedures. This book offers no advice on diving techniques (that's your instructor's job), and does not recommend that you deviate from any of the instructions for proper use of the tables. However, many diving authorities suggest that sport divers not closely approach the no-decompression limits, even when using the official procedures. A very hot shower may be all that's needed to enlarge bubbles to dangerous size if already present.

You can probably think of half a dozen good reasons for not trying to get the maximum available bottom time on every dive. Here are a few that are particularly relevant to sport divers:

First, the U.S. Navy tables were developed through dives conducted by young and healthy male military divers. Sport divers do not necessarily fit the same mold. There is some evidence that increasing age and obesity predispose divers toward decompression sickness. The question has been raised whether female divers are more susceptible to bends than are males, but the final results are not yet in. Furthermore, many authorities are concerned that diving during pregnancy may expose the fetus to the risk of decompression sickness.

Second, sport divers are typically remote from hyperbaric medical facilities (i.e., recompression chambers and doctors trained to manage diving accidents). Most professional divers dive very conservative profiles, and often have recompression chambers on site. What constitutes an acceptable risk to a commercial diver with a large supply of emergency oxygen, a recompression chamber, and a diving medical officer available may not be an acceptable risk to a sport diver at a resort. These should be lessons to all sport divers from those who make a living underwater.

Third, there is a small — but not negligible — incidence of bends using the U.S. Navy tables exactly as they were designed. Even Navy units see some decompression sickness, despite the fact that dives are generally line-tended and timed from the surface, with decompression stages suspended in the water at the proper depth, highly accurate depth gauges, etc. The U.S. Navy tables are too often accepted as gospel, and most divers believe that if you follow them you can't get bent. That's just not true. They are very safe when used as directed, but not 100 percent safe. "Bounce dives," i.e., short, deep dives following long dives (often made to free anchors that have become hung up on the bottom) are notorious for causing bends, for example. You should also be aware that there are different tables and procedures in use around the world, and that some of these tables are more conservative than the U.S. Navy tables. Several of them provide 5 to 10 minutes less bottom time for no-decompression dives at most depths, while others recommend much slower ascent rates.

Finally, recent research has shown that after no-decompression dives, divers often have nitrogen bubbles in their tissues which cause no clinical symptoms, even if the divers are well within the no-decompression limits. Whether or not bends symptoms are felt, these so-called "silent bubbles" are frequently present. Silent bubble formation appears to differ tremendously among individuals. This discovery suggests strongly that reducing your bottom time is cheap insurance. The line that divides silent bubbles from decompression sickness may be fuzzy, indeed.

In addition, the research provides another inducement to wait longer than the prescribed minimum time before flying after diving. Remember the drill the cabin attendants on an airliner always do regarding the oxygen masks that are supposed to flop down if you need them? Although commercial aircraft rarely lose their cabin pressure, it does happen. When it does, the sudden pressure drop frequently bends non-divers on board. In fact, the loss of cabin pressure is sometimes called (in military jargon) "explosive decompression!" If you've still got some excess nitrogen — or even some silent bubbles — rattling around in your body from your last dive, the pressure drop may induce more bubbles to form and enlarge. If you get bent along with the other passengers, your problems may not go away when theirs do after cabin pressure is restored, since you've got more nitrogen to worry about. How about spending an extra day on the beach to get that tan you missed by being under water?

There are lots of ways to get plenty of time under water and still be on the safe side of the tables. If you plan repetitive dives the proper way, with your deepest dive first, you'll maximize the amount of bottom time you get and minimize your surface intervals. If you apply the no-decompression limits to submerged time instead of bottom time, you'll have the same amount of time underwater, and only lose a minute or two at depth, compared to bottom time. You can also stop for several minutes at 10′ at the end of a dive, and include the stop in your bottom time as a safety precaution. If you include a safety stop within submerged time, and restrict submerged time to the no-decompression limit, you'll still be within the limit when you hit the surface. Consider reducing your no-decompression limits. Chances are, your diving instructor uses one of these safety procedures already.

SECTION 1. Basic Concepts and Single Dives

1.1 Bottom Time, No-decompression Limits, and No-decompression Dives

Example and Explanation

The no-decompression limit for 35' is ___*3/0*___ minutes.

Look up the no-decompression limits by depth in the table called "No-decompression Limits and Repetitive Group Designation Table." This is the first table you use. Most sets of tables (and this book) show no-decompression limits and bottom times in minutes rather than hours: minutes (e.g., 310 rather than 5:10). Be sure to use a set of tables that reads depth in feet (e.g., 35') rather than meters (e.g., 10m) for the problems in this book.

Questions

A. Bottom time is the amount of time between leaving the _____ to begin a _____ , and leaving the _____ to begin an _____.

B. No-decompression limits are the _____ amount of _____ _____ you may spend on a no-decompression dive to a given depth.

C. A no-decompression dive is a dive from which you can return _____ to the surface without making any _____ _____ at intermediate depths.

D. No-decompression limits decrease with increasing _____.

E. You should not exceed the _____ - _____ _____ for any sport dive.

F. The no-decompression limits are not defined for dives shallower than _____ , but you should not exceed the maximum time listed in the table for these shallow dives.

Problems

1. The no-decompression limit for 30′ is _____.

2. The no-decompression limit for 40′ is _____.

3. The no-decompression limit for 60′ is _____.

4. The no-decompression limit for 90′ is _____.

5. The no-decompression limit for]20′ is _____.

1.2 Depths and Dive Profiles

Example and Explanation

You spend 10 minutes at 45′ and then descend to 80′ for 15 minutes more. The dive is considered a single _25 min._ dive at _80′_ , which has a no-decompression limit of _40 min._.

   The maximum depth attained on the dive is 80′, and the bottom time on the dive is 10 + 15 = 25 minutes. Intermediate depths do not determine the no-decompression limit on a dive; the maximum depth does.

Questions

A. The depth of a dive is the _____ depth attained during the dive, measured in feet of seawater. The proper depth measurement is taken at the diver's _____, according to the U.S. Navy Manual.

B. On any dive, the no-decompression limit which applies is the one for the _____ depth attained.

Problems

1. You spend 15 minutes at 100′ and then ascend to 40′ for 10 minutes more. The dive is considered a single _____-minute dive at _____′, which has a no-decompression limit of _____.

2. You spend 23 minutes at 60′ and then ascend to 25′ for 20 minutes more. The dive is considered a single _____-minute dive at _____′, which has a no-decompression limit of _____.

3. You spend 40 minutes at 30′ and then descend to 70′ for 10 minutes more. The dive is considered a single _____-minute dive at _____′, which has a no-decompression limit of _____.

4. You spend 5 minutes at 110′ and then ascend to 52′ for 15 minutes more. The dive is considered a single _____-minute dive at _____′, which has a no-decompression limit of _____.

5. You spend 10 minutes at 100′, then ascend to 47′ for 10 minutes more, then ascend to 25′ for 5 minutes more. The dive is considered a single _____-minute dive at _____′, which has a no-decompression limit of _____.

1.3 Ascent Rate and Submerged Time

Example and Explanation

A 60′ dive with a 60-minute bottom time has a submerged time of _**61:00**_ which includes an ascent time of _**4:00**_.

Submerged time includes both bottom time and ascent time. At the correct ascent rate, an ascent will take 1 second per foot of depth. The 60-minute bottom time + (60′ × 1′/second = 1 minute) = 61 minutes.

Note: Ascent times and submerged times are shown as minutes: seconds in this book, per U.S. Navy Manual procedures.

Questions

A. Submerged time includes both _____ time and _____ time.

B. The correct normal ascent rate is _____/minute.

C. If submerged time is used instead of bottom time on a dive to the full no-decompression limit, bottom time will be _____ because of the time spent while _____.

Note: Many sport divers use submerged time (rather than bottom time) as a safety factor on no-decompression dives. Some sets of tables also include this recommendation. Most automatic, depth-activated dive timers show submerged time, not bottom time, since they don't stop running until near the end of an ascent. For the problems in this book, however, use bottom time unless specifically asked for submerged time.

Problems

1. A 60' dive with a 30-minute bottom time has a total submerged time of _____ , which includes an ascent time of _____ .

2. A 90' dive with a 30-minute bottom time has a total submerged time of _____ , which includes an ascent time of _____ .

3. A 120' dive with a 10-minute bottom time has a total submerged time of _____ , which includes an ascent time of _____ .

4. A 120' dive with a 20-minute bottom time has a total submerged time of _____ , which includes an ascent time of _____ .

5. A 30' dive with a 73-minute bottom time has a total submerged time of _____ , which includes an ascent time of _____ .

1.4 No-Decompression Limits for Non-Tabled Depths

Example and Explanation

The no-decompression limit for a dive to 53' is _60 min._ .

   A depth of 53' is not listed in the tables. There are no depths listed between 50' and 60'. You must use the no-decompression limit for the *next greater* tabled depth (60' in this example) when diving to a non-tabled depth.

Questions

A. Non-tabled depths are not specifically _____ in the tables.

B. On a dive to a non-tabled depth, the applicable no-decompression limit is that for the next _____ tabled depth; do not interpolate (i.e., attempt to estimate non-tabled numbers).

Problems

1. The no-decompression limit for a dive to 41' is _____ .

2. The no-decompression limit for a dive to 49' is _____ .

3. The no-decompression limit for a dive to 65' is _____ .

4. The no-decompression limit for a dive to 88' is _____ .

5. The no-decompression limit for a dive to 54' is _____ .

COMMENTS

That wasn't hard, was it? You've learned most of the rules for single no-decompression dives; how to define bottom and submerged times; and what to do if your dive includes more than one depth level. You can determine the maximum bottom time available on single no-decompression dives. Next, you'll learn how a first dive affects bottom time on a second dive.

SECTION 2: Repetitive Dive Concepts and Two-Dive Problems

2.1 Introduction to Repetitive Groups

Example and Explanation

At the end of an 80' dive for 10 minutes, you will be in repetitive group ___C___.

  Look up repetitive group designators in the same table you used for no-decompression limits. Find the depth of the dive, and then work along that depth line until you come to the correct bottom time. The repetitive group designator letters are along the edge of the table. The one matching your bottom time is your repetitive group. For convenience, we'll call a "repetitive group" a "group," or just give the letter of the group.

Questions

A. A repetitive group designator is a letter that indicates the amount of excess _____ that you have dissolved in your body.

B. The repetitive group you are in at the end of a dive is higher (calling A the low end of the alphabet and Z the high end) the longer your _____ _____ , for any given depth.

C. The repetitive group you are in at the end of a dive will be higher the _____ your depth, for any given bottom time.

D. Shorter _____ dives may put you in the same group as longer shallow dives.

Problems

1. At the end of a 40' dive for 30 minutes, you are in group _____.

2. At the end of a 40' dive for 50 minutes, you are in group _____.

20

3. At the end of a 60′ dive for 30 minutes, you are in group _____.

4. At the end of a 60′ dive for 50 minutes, you are in group _____.

5. At the end of a 25′ dive for 55 minutes, you are in group _____.

2.2 Repetitive Groups for Non-Tabled Depths and Times

Examples and Explanations

At the end of a 40′ dive for 51 minutes, you are in group ___*G*___.

The tables list 40′, but they don't show a bottom time of 51 minutes. They list 50 and 70 minutes. Since bottom time exceeds 50 minutes, use the next longer tabled time (70 minutes) to find your group.

At the end of a 41′ dive for 50 minutes, you are in group ___*G*___.

The tables list 40′ and 50′, but not 41′. Since your depth exceeds 40′, you use the next greater tabled depth (50′) to find your group.

Questions

A. Non-tabled times are not specifically _____ in the tables.

B. For non-tabled depths, you should use the next _____ tabled depth to find your group; do not interpolate.

C. For non-tabled bottom times, you should use the next _____ tabled time to find your group; do not interpolate.

Problems

1. At the end of a dive to 70′ for 30 minutes, you are in group _____.

2. At the end of a dive to 70′ for 31 minutes, you are in group _____.

3. At the end of a dive to 70′ for 40 minutes, you are in group _____.

4. At the end of a dive to 72′ for 40 minutes, you are in group _____.

5. At the end of a dive to 91′ for 23 minutes, you are in group _____.

2.3 Surface Intervals

Examples and Explanations

If you are in group G at the end of a dive, you'll be in group D if you begin your next dive after a surface interval of __2:00__ or in group C if you begin your next dive after a surface interval of __2:59__.

Use the Surface Interval Credit Table to find out what group you are in after a surface interval. Surface Interval Credit tables usually show time in hours:minutes. We'll do the same, per U.S. Navy Manual procedure. (Surface interval times look like ascent and submerged times, but ascent and submerged times read in minutes:seconds, rather than hours:minutes.) For most sets of tables, enter the Surface Interval Credit table on the line corresponding to your group. Move along the line until you come to the first box whose tabled minimum time equals or exceeds your surface interval. Finally, turn 90° at that box, and exit the table, noting your new group at the edge of the table. As a group G diver, a surface interval of between 2:00 and 2:58 puts you into group D. A surface interval of between 2:59 and 4:25 puts you into group C.

If you are in group L at the end of a dive, you will be in group __G__ after a minimum surface interval of 1:50 and in group __D__ after a minimum surface interval of 3:37.

This example shows you how to figure out how long you may have to wait to get into another group. To solve this kind of problem easily, move into the Surface Interval Credit Table from two directions simultaneously, along the L line (for starting group) and along the G line (for end group). They intersect at the box showing 1:50–2:19. That means that if you end a dive in group L, you'll be in group G after a surface interval of between 1:50 and 2:19. Similarly, the L (starting) and D (ending) lines intersect at 3:37–4:35. You'll be in group D after a minimum surface interval of 3:37, and remain in D until your surface interval exceeds 4:35.

Questions

A. A surface interval is the time between _____ after one dive and beginning your _____ for the next dive. If the surface interval is long enough, you may change groups before the next dive.

B. The longer your surface interval, the lower your _____ at the end of the interval.

22

C. To move to a new group, your surface interval must equal or _____ the minimum time listed in the Surface Interval Credit Table for that group.

Problems

1. If you are in group C at the end of a dive, you will be in group B after a minimum surface interval of _____ and in group A after a minimum surface interval of _____.

2. If you are in group F at the end of a dive, you will be in group D after a minimum surface interval of _____ and in group B after a minimum surface interval of _____.

3. If you are in group G at the end of a dive, you will be in group C after a minimum surface interval of _____ and in group B after a minimum surface interval of _____.

4. If you are in group H at the end of a dive, you will be in group _____ after a minimum surface interval of 3:20, and in group _____ after a minimum surface interval of 4:00.

5. If you are in group L at the end of a dive, you will be in group _____ after a minimum surface interval of 0:15, and in group _____ after a minimum surface interval of 0:25.

2.4 Minimum and Maximum Surface Intervals

Examples and Explanations

You surface after a first dive with a bottom time of 15 minutes at 80′. You remain on the surface for 0:08 and then descend again to 80′. Your bottom time must not exceed _25 min._ on the second dive.

Since your surface interval between dives was not at least 0:10, the second dive is just a continuation of the first dive. You don't have to include the surface interval in the bottom time, but you do have to sum the bottom times for the two dives. The no-decompression limit for 80′ is 40 minutes. Since you've used up 15 minutes on the first dive, your bottom time must not exceed 25 minutes (15 + 25 = 40) on the second dive.

If you are in group J, you must have a minimum surface interval of _8:41_ to reach group A, and minimum surface interval of _12:01_ before another dive would not be considered a repetitive dive.

If you end a dive in group J, you'll be in group A after a surface interval of 8:41–12:00. The table only lists times up to 12:00, after which you are no longer considered to have any excess residual nitrogen.

Questions

A. Unless your surface interval is at least _____ , a subsequent dive is considered a continuation of the _____ dive, and the no-decompression limit that applies is that for the _____ depth attained on either submergence.

B. After any no-decompression dive, a surface interval exceeding _____ is required to be no longer in a repetitive group.

Problems

1. You surface after a first dive of 20 minutes at 70', remain on the surface for 0:07, and then descend again to a maximum of 70'. Your bottom time must not exceed _____ on the second dive.

2. You surface after a first dive of 45 minutes at 60', remain on the surface for 0:07, and then descend again to a maximum of 40'. Your bottom time must not exceed _____ on the second dive.

3. If you end a dive in group D, you must have a minimum surface interval of _____ before reaching group A, and a minimum surface interval of _____ before another dive would not be considered repetitive.

4. If you end a dive in group B, you must have a minimum surface interval of _____ before reaching group A.

5. If you end a dive in group A, you must have a minimum surface interval of _____ before another dive would not be considered repetitive.

2.5 Residual Nitrogen Times and Repetitive Dives

Example and Explanation

If you are in group F, you have a residual nitrogen time (RNT) of _36 min._ on a repetitive dive to 60'.

You can find RNT on the Repetitive Dive Timetable. RNT is shown on most sets of tables (and in this book) as minutes rather than hours:minutes. Enter the table on the line corresponding to your group, and move along the line until you come to the box on the line corresponding to the intended depth of your next dive; the box shows your RNT. If your table has two numbers per box, be sure to read the correct number for RNT, and ignore the other number for now. You'll find 36 at the intersection of the F line and the 60' line.

Questions

A. Residual nitrogen time (RNT) is the amount of time you must consider you have already spent on the bottom at the beginning of any _____ dive.

B. The length of your RNT depends on what _____ you are in at the start of a repetitive dive and on the _____ of a repetitive dive.

C. Lower groups have _____ RNT on repetitive dives to any given depth.

Problems

1. In group F, your RNT is _____ on a repetitive dive to 50′.

2. In group F, your RNT is _____ on a repetitive dive to 90′.

3. In group D, your RNT is _____ on a repetitive dive to 60′.

4. In group B, your RNT is _____ on a repetitive dive to 60′.

5. In group C, your RNT is _____ on a repetitive dive to 100′.

2.6 Actual and Total Bottom Times

Example and Explanation

If you are in group E and make a dive to 60′ for 20 minutes, your RNT is _30 min._, your actual bottom time (ABT) is _20 min._, your total bottom time (TBT) is _50 min._, and you are in group _H_ at the end of the dive.

A group E diver has an RNT of 30 minutes at 60′. RNT + ABT = TBT, so 30 + 20 = 50. Return to the No-decompression Limits and Repetitive Group Designation Table, using TBT as if you were making a first dive. A 60′, 50-minute dive puts you in group H.

Note: TBT is sometimes called "equivalent single dive time" in U.S. Navy terminology. Equivalent single dive time better describes the situation, but is not as commonly used by sports divers as TBT. They mean the same thing. An easy mnemonic to remember the various kinds of bottom time is "RAT": Residual plus Actual equals Total.

Questions

A. Actual bottom time (ABT) is the amount of bottom time actually used on _____ dive.

B. To determine your group at the end of a repetitive dive, use your _____ _____ time as if you had made a single dive for that amount of time.

C. Total bottom time (TBT) is the sum of _____ _____ time and _____ bottom time.

Problems

1. If you are in group D and make a dive to 60′ for 31 minutes, your RNT is _____ , your ABT is _____ , your TBT is _____ , and you are in group _____ at the end of the repetitive dive.

2. If you are in group E and make a dive to 90′ for 8 minutes, your RNT is _____ , your ABT is _____ , your TBT is _____ , and you are in group _____ at the end of the repetitive dive.

3. If you are in group A and make a dive to 60′ for 31 minutes, your RNT is _____ , your ABT is _____ , your TBT is _____ , and you are in group _____ at the end of the repetitive dive.

4. If you are in Group E and make a dive to 70′ for 19 minutes, your RNT is _____ , your ABT is _____ , your TBT is _____ , and you are in group _____ at the end of the repetitive dive.

5. If you are in group H and make a dive to 70′ for 5 minutes, your RNT is _____ , your ABT is _____ , your TBT is _____ , and you are in group _____ at the end of the repetitive dive.

2.7 Maximum Actual Bottom Times on Repetitive Dives

Example and Explanation

If you start a repetitive dive in group F, you have an ABT_{max} of _24 min._ at 60'.

ABT_{max} is the maximum actual bottom time (ABT) available on any dive. On single dives, ABT_{max} = the no-decompression limit. On repetitive dives, ABT_{max} = the no-decompression limit minus RNT. For this reason, ABT_{max} is sometimes called the "adjusted no-decompression limit" or "adjusted maximum no-decompression bottom time" for repetitive dives. As a group F diver, your RNT at 60' = 36 minutes. The no-decompression limit for 60' is 60 minutes. RNT + ABT = TBT, or TBT − RNT = ABT. TBT must not exceed the no-decompression limit, so TBT − RNT = ABT_{max} = 60 − 36 = 24. Some sets of tables have done this calculation for you. Remember the second number in the box next to RNT? That number is ABT_{max}. Some tables do not even show RNT, just ABT_{max}.

Questions

A. Maximum actual bottom time (ABT_{max}) on any no-decompression dive is the _____ amount of ABT available. ABT_{max} is determined by subtracting the _____ _____ _____ from the _____ - _____ _____ for any given depth.

B. ABT_{max} plus RNT (if any) is equal to the _____ - _____ _____ for any given depth.

Problems

1. If you are in group F, your ABT_{max} is _____ on a dive to 50'.

2. If you are in group F, your ABT_{max} is _____ on a dive to 90'.

3. If you are in group D, your ABT_{max} is _____ on a dive to 60'.

4. If you are in group B, your ABT_{max} is _____ on a dive to 60'.

5. If you are in group D, your ABT_{max} is _____ on a dive to 100'.

2.8 Maximum Depths on Repetitive Dives

Example and Explanation

If you are in group J and intend to make a no-decompression dive for 30 minutes, you must not exceed a depth of ___40'___.

At increasing depths, RNT approaches—and then exceeds—the no-decompression limits. ABT_{max} then goes to 0, and it is not possible to make a no-decompression dive. The RNT for group J at 40' is 116 minutes, leaving an ABT_{max} of 84 minutes (200 − 116 = 84). The 30 - minute dive in the example is possible. However, RNT for group J for a 50' dive is 87 minutes, leaving an ABT_{max} of only 13 minutes. For group J, the RNT for 60' is 70 minutes. This means that as soon as a group J diver descended past 50', he would already be 10 minutes over the no-decompression limit!

Questions

A. ABT_{max} sometimes can be _____ than the amount of time required to make a dive.

B. For any given group, RNT gets closer and closer to the _____ - _____ _____ with increasing _____.

Problems

1. If you are in group H and intend to make a no-decompression 15-minute dive, you must not exceed a depth of _____.

2. If you are in group K and intend to make a no-decompression 25-minute dive, you must not exceed a depth of _____.

3. If you are in group B and intend to make a no-decompression 50-minute dive, you must not exceed a depth of _____.

4. If you are in group C and intend to make a no-decompression 10-minute dive, you must not exceed a depth of _____.

5. If you are in group E and intend to make a no-decompression 15-minute dive, you must not exceed a depth of _____.

2.9 The Exception Rule

Example and Explanation

After a 50′ dive for 60 minutes and a surface interval of 0:25, your ABT_{max} on a second dive to 50′ would be ___*40 min.*___.

At the end of a 50′ dive for 60 minutes, you are in group H. After a surface interval of 0:25, you are still in group H, and have an RNT of 66 minutes on a repetitive dive to 50′. If you use the RNT for group H, you have only 34 minutes ABT_{max} ($100 - 66 = 34$). According to the exception rule, you may instead use an RNT equal to the ABT of the first dive—60 minutes. In this case, your ABT_{max} is 40 minutes at 50′ (rather than 34 minutes) on the second dive. When a repetitive dive is to the same or greater depth than the previous dive, the RNT for the repetitive dive may be longer than the ABT of the previous dive. In this event, you may add the ABT of the previous dive to the ABT of the repetitive dive to obtain an equivalent single dive time for the maximum depth attained on either dive.

Note: Using the exception rule is usually less conservative than using the Repetitive Dive Timetable. In the example above, the exception rule provides 6 more minutes of bottom time. The Repetitive Dive Timetable has a safety factor built in for most dives. For the problems below, use whichever method gives the greatest ABT_{max}. In some cases, the exception rule may not provide as much bottom time as the Repetitive Dive Timetable.

Questions

A. The exception rule permits you to use _____ bottom time on one dive as _____ _____ time for a subsequent dive.

B. The exception rule can only be applied when a repetitive dive is to the _____ or _____ depth than the previous dive.

Problems

1. After an 80′ dive for 20 minutes and a surface interval of 0:10, your ABT_{max} on a second dive to 80′ would be _____.

2. After a 90′ dive for 20 minutes and a surface interval of 0:30, your ABT_{max} on a second dive to 90′ would be _____.

3. After a 60′ dive for 35 minutes and a surface interval of 0:17, your ABT_{max} on a second dive to 80′ would be _____.

4. After a 70′ dive for 38 minutes and a surface interval of 0:22, your ABT_{max} on a second dive to 80′ would be _____.

5. After an 82′dive for 25 minutes and a surface interval of 0:10, your ABT_{max} on a second dive to 70′ would be _____.

2.10 Residual Nitrogen Times for Shallow Dives

Note: There are two popular methods for assigning groups and RNT for repetitive dives to 35′ or less. If your set of tables does not show RNT for depths shallower than 40′, use Method 1 to solve the problems. If your set shows RNT for all depths, use Method 2. The Appendix gives a detailed explanation of how either method can be used on any set of tables.

Examples and Explanations

(Method 1): If you're in group C and begin a dive to 30′, your RNT is _25 min._ , and after an ABT of 50 minutes, your TBT is _75min._ and you're in group __H__.

For Method 1, the RNT at the start of the shallow dive is that which would apply to a 40′ dive. A group C diver has an RNT of 25 minutes at 40′. Since your ABT is 50 minutes, your TBT is 75 minutes. After the shallow dive, use your TBT to determine what group you would be in if you had made a 40′ dive. A TBT of 75 minutes at 40′ puts you in group H.

(Method 2): If you're in group C and begin a dive to 30′, your RNT is _45 min._, and after an ABT of 50 minutes, your TBT is _95 min._ and you're in group __F__.

For Method 2, follow the same procedure that you would use for any other depth. The example is self-explanatory.

Problems

1. If you're in group B and begin a dive to 25', your RNT is _____ , and after an ABT of 60 minutes, your TBT is _____ and you're in group _____.

2. If you're in group D and begin a dive to 35', your RNT is _____ , and after an ABT of 48 minutes, your TBT is _____ and you're in group _____.

3. If you're in group E and begin a dive to 20', your RNT is _____ , and after an ABT of 75 minutes, your TBT is _____ and you're in group _____.

4. If you're in group C and begin a dive to 15', your RNT is _____ , and after an ABT of 30 minutes, your TBT is _____ and you're in group _____.

5. If you're in group A and begin a dive to 10', your RNT is _____ , and after an ABT of 49 minutes, your TBT is _____ and you're in group _____.

COMMENTS

Congratulations! The hard part's over. You've learned nearly all of the basic procedures you need for no-decompression repetitive diving. The deeper you go and the longer you stay, the more dissolved nitrogen you pick up in your tissues. The no-decompression limit for each depth has been calculated to keep that nitrogen within safe bounds. When you surface, you are assigned a repetitive group. The higher the group, the more nitrogen. On any dive within 12 hours of a previous dive, you have to take the excess nitrogen into account, which means that when you start your next descent you are considered to have already spent some time at depth. This residual nitrogen time (RNT) is added to your actual bottom time (ABT) on the repetitive dive to determine total bottom time (TBT) for the dive.

You cannot stay for the full no-decompression limit on a repetitive dive because of the residual nitrogen from the previous dive. The maximum length of your dive is shortened by the RNT. The maximum ABT you can spend on a no-decompression repetitive dive is called ABT_{max}. Within any group, RNT (and ABT_{max}) differ depending on the depth of the intended dive. The higher the group, the greater the RNT and the less ABT_{max}. The TBT for a no-decompression dive must not exceed the no-decompression limit. For no-decompression dives, ABT_{max} plus RNT equals the no-decompression limit.

While on the surface between dives, you begin to lose the excess nitrogen, and move from higher to lower groups. You must stay on the surface at least 10 minutes, or both dives are considered to be two parts of a single dive, with a single bottom time equivalent to the sum of both parts. The longer the surface interval, the lower your group when you begin the next dive. Your group on the next dive is thus affected by the length and depth of the previous dive, and the length of your surface interval.

SECTION 3: Three-and Four-Dive Problems

In this section, you're going to solve three- and four-dive no-decompression problems. There's really no difference between figuring out two-dive problems and multi-dive problems. After any first dive, the same basic routine is followed. Determine: (1) your group upon surfacing; (2) your group after any surface interval; (3) your RNT; and (4) your ABT_{max} for a second dive. After the second (or third, or fourth) dive, you do exactly the same thing, using TBT to determine your group upon surfacing.

So that we don't have to write out dive profiles in words, we'll describe each dive by giving the depth in feet, a slash (/), and then the ABT in minutes. The wedge symbol ▼ marks the start of each dive in a sequence: ▼ 100'/15" means "a first dive to 100' for an ABT of 15 minutes." If the wedge is preceded by a letter, it's a repetitive dive and the diver is in the group indicated by the letter: "B— ▼ 60'/10" means "a repetitive dive, starting in group B, to 60' for an ABT of 10 minutes." Any letter right after a dive means the diver is in that group at the end of the dive. Remember, bottom times and RNT's are always given in whole minutes, and surface intervals and submerged times are always given in hours:minutes.

For repetitive dive problems, the sequence looks like this: ▼ depth/ABT for first dive—group at the end of the dive—surface interval—group at the start of the next dive— ▼ depth/ABT for next dive—group—, and so forth. For example, "▼ 100'/15—E—1:00—D— ▼ 70'/30—J" means "a 100' dive for 15 minutes ABT puts you in group E; a 1:00 surface interval moves you into group D; a 70' dive for 30 minutes ABT then puts you into group J."

Instructions: In most of the problems, you'll see a sequence with one or more blanks to fill in. Follow these instructions very carefully, and you'll probably get all of the problems right the first time.

1. When you are asked for a depth, use the *maximum* depth permitted by the given ABT for a no-decompression dive. For example, the correct answer for "▼ _____/20" is 110'; the correct answer for "D— ▼ _____/ 30" is 70'.

2. When you are asked for a bottom time, use ABT_{max} for that depth. For example, the correct answer for "▼ 100'/ _____" is 25 minutes. If it's a repetitive dive, don't forget to take RNT into account. For instance, the correct answer for "D— ▼ 100'/_____" is 11 minutes. When a prob-

lem already shows a bottom time next to a depth, it will always be ABT (keep in mind that a given ABT may or may not be ABT_{max}).

3. When you are asked for a surface interval, use the *minimum* surface interval that will put you into the desired group. For example, the correct answer for "D _____ C" is 1:10.

If you know the depth and ABT for a dive, you then can figure out the RNT, TBT, and appropriate groups before and after the dive. However, you won't have to put down RNT or TBT for any of the problems unless specifically requested.

3.1 Three-Dive Bottom Time Problems

Example and Explanation

▼ 100'/_**25**____—H—2:23—E— ▼ 100'/_**7**____—H—2:45—D— ▼ 70'/_**30**___—J

To get started on these problems, first insert ABT_{max} (which is the no-decompression limit for single dives, of course) for the first dive. Then proceed on the sequence given above. In the example, a first dive of 100' has a no-decompression limit of 25 minutes, putting you in group H. After a 2:23 surface interval, you move to group E. As an E diver, you have an RNT of 18 minutes on a 100' dive, and an ABT_{max} of 7 minutes. Your TBT is 25 minutes (as in the first dive, where RNT = 0, ABT = 25, and TBT = 25), and you are in group H. After a surface interval of 2:45, you are in group D. As a D diver, you have a 20 minute RNT on a 70' dive, and an ABT_{max} of 30 minutes. Your TBT is 50 minutes, putting you in group J.

Problems

1. ▼ 90'/_____—H—2:24—D— ▼ 80'/_____—I—1:00—G— ▼ 70'/_____—J

2. ▼ 80'/_____—I—1:00—G— ▼ 60'/_____—J—1:20—G— ▼ 50'/_____—L

3. ▼ 85'/_____—H—1:00—G— ▼ 65'/_____—J—1:47—G— ▼ 45'/_____—L

4. ▼ 70'/_____ —J—3:05—D— ▼ 70'/_____ —J—1:48—F—
   ▼ 60'/_____ —J

5. ▼ 50'/_____ —L—4:36—C— ▼ 50'/_____ —L—1:49—H—
   ▼ 40'/_____ —N

3.2 Four-Dive Bottom Time Problems

Example and Explanation

▼ 107'/_20_ — _G_ —1:45— _E_ — ▼ 55'/_30_ —J—
0:20— _J_ — ▼ 47'/_13_ — _L_ —2:00— _G_ —
▼ 25'/60— _L_ (Method 1) or _I_ (Method 2)

These problems are just like the problems in 3.1, except that you have to fill in the repetitive groups yourself. In the example, a 107' first dive has an ABT_{max} equal to the no-decompression limit for 110', 20 minutes. This puts you in group G. After a surface interval of 1:45, you move into group E.

The second dive is considered a 60' dive, for which you have an RNT of 30 minutes and an ABT_{max} of 30 minutes. After the second dive, you are in group J. A surface interval of 0:20 still leaves you in group J. The third dive is considered a 50' dive, for which you have an RNT of 87 minutes and an ABT_{max} of 13 minutes.

After the third dive, you are in group L. Following a 2:00 surface interval, you move to group G. In group G, for a 25' dive, if you use Method 1 (see Problem Set 2.10) you have an RNT of 73 minutes and an ABT of 60 minutes, giving you a TBT of 133 minutes and putting you in group L. If you use Method 2 you have an RNT of 160 minutes, giving you a TBT of 220 minutes and putting you in group I.

Problems

1. ▼ 50'/_____ —_____ —4:36—_____ — ▼ 50'/_____ —
   _____ —1:49—_____ — ▼ 40'/_____ —_____ —1:30—
   _____ — ▼ 40'/_____ —_____

2. ▼ 70'/_____ —_____ —1:30—_____ — ▼ 56'/_____ —
   _____ —0:45—_____ — ▼ 41'/_____ —_____ —0:10—
   _____ — ▼ 30'/60 —_____

3. ▼ 95'/_____ —_____ —2:30—_____ — ▼ 82'/_____ —
_____ —0:40—_____ — ▼ 66'/_____ —_____ —0:19—
_____ — ▼ 41'/_____ —_____

4. ▼ 111'/_____ —_____ —3:56—_____ — ▼ 91'/_____
—_____ —5:00—_____ — ▼ 73'/_____ —_____ —1:50
—_____ — ▼ 60'/_____ —_____

5. ▼ 44'/_____ —_____ —6:15—_____ — ▼ 59'/_____ —
_____ —0:20—_____ — ▼ 42'/_____ —_____ —3:17—
_____ — ▼ 20'/30—_____

3.3 Surface Intervals for Preselected Repetitive Dives

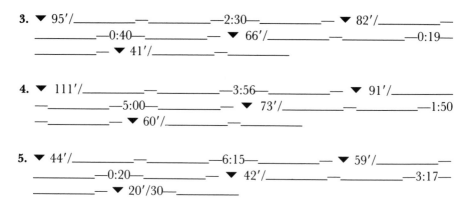

Example and Explanation

▼ 100'/25— *H* — *1:42* — *E* — ▼ 90'/10— *H*
— *3:21* — *C* — ▼ 80'/27

These problems are easy if you ask yourself: (1) What group you need to be in at the start of a repetitive dive; and (2) How long a surface interval is required to get to that group from the one you were in at the end of the previous dive. This situation is one of the most common you'll encounter on dive trips. For instance, after a first dive, you may want to shoot a roll of film on the second dive. You know it takes more than 10 minutes to do the job, and the water will be 90' deep. How long do you have to stay on the surface before the second dive? In the example above, after a first dive of 100'/25, you want to make a 90' no-decompression repetitive dive of at least 10 minutes, followed by an 80' no-decompression repetitive dive for at least 25 minutes. At the end of the first dive, you're in group H.

At the start of the second dive you must be in a group with an RNT at 90' of no more than 20 minutes to get an ABT_{max} of at least 10 minutes, since TBT at 90' may not exceed 30 minutes. You must therefore get from group H to group E, which requires a minimum surface interval of 1:42. At the end of the second dive, you're back in group H.

At the start of the third dive you must be in a group with an RNT at 80' of no more than 15 minutes, or an ABT_{max} of at least 25 minutes. You therefore have to get into group C. The minimum surface interval for the change from H to C is 3:21, and your ABT_{max} is 27 minutes at 80'.

Problems

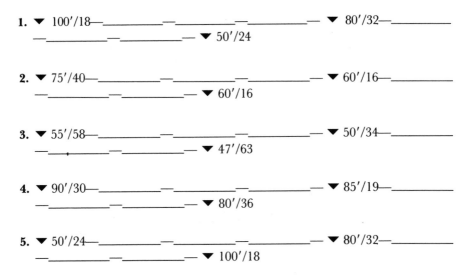

1. ▼ 100'/18———————— —————————— ————————— — ▼ 80'/32—————————
—————————— —————————— — ▼ 50'/24

2. ▼ 75'/40———————— —————————— ————————— — ▼ 60'/16—————————
—————————— —————————— — ▼ 60'/16

3. ▼ 55'/58———————— —————————— ————————— — ▼ 50'/34—————————
—— , ———————— —————————— — ▼ 47'/63

4. ▼ 90'/30———————— —————————— ————————— — ▼ 85'/19—————————
—————————— —————————— — ▼ 80'/36

5. ▼ 50'/24———————— —————————— ————————— — ▼ 80'/32—————————
—————————— —————————— — ▼ 100'/18

Note: Problems 1 and 5 have the same ABT at the same depths, but in Problem 1, the deepest dive is first (the way it should be), and in Problem 5, the deepest dive is last. Notice the difference in the total surface interval for the two profiles. See why you should make the deepest dives first?

3.4 Preselected Repetitive Dives and Restricted Bottom Time on Previous Dives

---

Example and Explanation

▼ 80'/__30__ — __G__ —2:00— __D__ — ▼ 60'/35— __J__
—2:00— __F__ — ▼ __50__ '/30

What if your second dive is going to be in a fine spot where you want maximum bottom time, but you don't want to miss a good first dive. You're on a half-day charter boat where your surface interval is limited. You'll have to compromise by restricting your first dive. In this example, you want an ABT on your second dive of at least 35 minutes at 60'. You must therefore not be higher than a group D diver (RNT 24 minutes, ABT_{max} 36 minutes). You anticipate a maximum surface interval of 2:00 between dives.

The easiest way to work this problem is to go "backwards" though the Surface Interval Credit Table from the end group side toward the starting

---

group side. Start at the side of the table that shows the group required at the *end* of the surface interval. Move inward along the line that ends with the required group (D). Notice that the minimum surface intervals in the boxes on that line decrease. When you come to the first box that includes your expected surface interval (2:00—2:58), turn 90° and move along a line toward the side that shows *starting* groups. The starting group on the edge of that line (G) is the highest group you can end a previous dive with, and still get into the group required for the next dive. You must be no higher than G at the end of the first dive, or you won't make it into D in 2:00. You now select some combination of depth and ABT that won't get you any higher than group G on your first dive. We've specified a depth to make it easy, but lots of different first dives, e.g., 100'/22, 90'/25, 80'/30, 70'/35, or 60'/40, will put you in G on your first dive.

How can you calculate your maximum depth for the third dive, if you want an ABT of at least 30 minutes? If you're in J after the second dive, and have a 2:00 surface interval, you can go as deep as 50' on the third dive, since you'll be a F diver with an ABT_{max} of 53 minutes at 50'. You can't do 60'/30 because the ABT_{max} for an F diver at 60' is only 24 minutes.

Problems

1. ▼ 100'/_____—_____—2:00—_____— ▼ 60'/35_____
   —2:00—_____—- ▼ _____/30

2. ▼ 103'/_____—_____—2:30—_____— ▼ 70'/30_____
   —1:00—_____— ▼ _____/34

3. ▼ 90'/_____—_____—0:45—_____— ▼ 70'/35_____
   —1:30—_____— ▼ _____/15

4. ▼ 75'/_____—_____—1:15—_____— ▼ 50'/60_____
   —2:00—_____— ▼ _____/60

5. ▼ 70'/_____—_____—1:40—_____— ▼ 55'/25_____
   —0:10—_____— ▼ _____/10

COMMENTS

If you've been able to solve all the problems in this section correctly, you know your way through the table like a pro. You can calculate ABT_{max} and maximum depth for any no-decompression dive in a sequence. You can also determine your repetitive group after each dive. You've learned how to figure out what group you must be in to make any no-decompression dive, and how to find the minimum surface interval necessary to get from one group to another. You also can work through the Surface Interval Credit table from either side. Once you know what group is required to make a particular dive and what your maximum surface interval will be before the dive, you can adjust the profile of the preceeding dive to be sure that it will be possible to make your next dive as planned.

Despite the best planning, unforseen events may sometimes force you into a situation where your TBT exceeds the no-decompression limit, or your ascent rate exceeds the normal rate. In these cases, you'll have to stop at one or more intermediate depths to release some of the excess nitrogen in your body before you can surface. The next section includes dive profiles that include decompression stops, as well as some related situations such as cold or strenuous dives, and flying after diving.

SECTION 4: Decompression Dives, Fast and Slow Ascents, Cold or Strenuous Dives, and High Altitudes After Diving

The U.S. Navy decompression tables are designed for a specific ascent rate which produces a controlled release of excess nitrogen on the way up. In some senses, the term "no-decompression dive" is a misnomer. Every dive includes a period of decompression during which the excess nitrogen decreases. On no-decompression dives, that period is during a direct ascent to the surface. On decompression dives, that period includes time spent ascending toward the surface, as well as time spent at decompression stops.

If your ascent is too fast, you subject yourself to a rapid pressure change, which increases the risk of decompression sickness. If you ascend too slowly or linger at depth at the end of your ABT_{max}, you dissolve more nitrogen in your body than you should while lingering at depth, and there is again an increased risk of bends. This section includes problem sets dealing with both types of variations in ascent rate.

The schedules in the tables are for dives under good—if not optimal—conditions. Under some circumstances such as very cold water or dives requiring strenuous work underwater, it is necessary to use a modified decompression procedure. One problem set in this section shows you how to allow for these circumstances.

You already know that as long as you're in a repetitive group, you have some excess dissolved nitrogen in your body. If you're diving the Navy tables, you're expected to lose this nitrogen gradually under one atmosphere of pressure while on the surface at sea level. If you get into an airplane or drive up a mountain, you'll be under less than sea-level pressure. This section concludes with problems related to leaving sea level after diving.

We'll highlight decompression stops with: [ ]. Stop times are in whole minutes (as for bottom times), except when fractions of minutes are required. Stop times are then shown as minutes:seconds. For example, [10'/15] means a decompression stop at 10' for 15 minutes, and [20'/2:30] means a stop of 20' for 2½ minutes.

4.1 Accidental Overstays at Depth

Example and Explanation

On a 100' repetitive dive as a C diver, your ABT is 18 minutes. You must stop at __10'__ for __3 min.__ before surfacing, and you are in group __I__ at the end of the dive. Shown schematically, C— ▼ 100'/18—[__10'/3__]—I.

Most sets of tables for sport divers include decompression stops and groups for the first few tabled times that exceed no-decompression limits. You can also find stops and groups in the U.S. Navy Standard Air Decompression Table. On the above dive, your RNT for group C at 100' is 10 minutes and your ABT is 18 minutes. TBT is 28 minutes, which exceeds the no-decompression limit. The next greater tabled bottom time is 30 minutes, which requires a 3-minute, 10' stop. The table also shows your group after the dive, next to the decompression schedule you used.

Questions

A. A decompression dive is any dive on which you cannot return _____ to the surface without making any _____ _____ at intermediate depths.

B. Decompression stops are made during an ascent, part way to the surface at a specified _____ (measured at a diver's _____) for a specified amount of _____.

C. It is necessary to make at least one decompression stop if your ABT (on first dives) or TBT (on repetitive dives) exceeds the _____ - _____ _____.

D. For non-tabled depths or bottom times, use the next _____ tabled depth or the next _____ tabled time to determine decompression stops: do not interpolate.

Problems

1. ▼ 80'/42—[_____/_____]—_____

2. ▼ 70'/60—[_____/_____]—_____

3. D— ▼ 81'/30—[_____/_____]—_____

4. C— ▼ 100'/20—[_____/_____]—_____

5. F— ▼ 60'/40—[_____/_____]—_____

4.2 Dives Which Accidentally Exceed Planned Depths

Example and Explanation

After a first dive of ▼ 60'/60 and a surface interval of 3:00, you begin a second dive planned for 60'. After an ABT of 29 minutes, you notice your depth gauge reads 65'. You should make a [_10'/8_] stop.

At the end of the first dive, you are in group J. After a surface interval of 3:00, you are in group E. Your RNT for 60' is 30 minutes, leaving an ABT_{max} of 30 minutes. Exceeding your planned depth puts you on the 70' schedule. The RNT for group E at 70' is 26 minutes. After an ABT of 29 minutes, your TBT is thus 55 minutes (29 + 26 = 55). This TBT exceeds the no-decompression limit for 70'. The next greater tabled time for 70' is 60 minutes, and requires a 10' stop for 8 minutes.

Questions

A. If you are near the no-decompression limit for a planned depth and accidentally exceed that depth, you probably will have to make a _____ _____ at a depth of _____ on the way up.

B. Some dive profiles require decompression stops at several _____ for various amounts of _____.

Problems

1. On a first dive planned for 90', after an ABT of 27 minutes, your depth gauge reads 92'. Your decompression stop(s) is/are _____.

2. After ▼ 110'/16 and a surface interval of 1:50, you begin a second dive planned for 80'. After an ABT of 23 minutes, you notice your depth gauge reads 91'. Your decompression stop(s) is/are _____.

3. After ▼ 85'/30 and a surface interval of 2:25, you begin a second dive planned for 70'. After an ABT of 30 minutes, you notice your depth gauge reads 80'. Your decompression stop(s) is/are _____.

4. On a first dive planned for 95', after an ABT of 25 minutes, your depth gauge reads 102'. Your decompression stop(s) is/are _____.

5. After ▼ 50'/70 and a surface interval of 1:10, you begin a second dive planned for 40'. After an ABT of 60 minutes, you notice your depth gauge reads 45'. Your decompression stop(s) is/are _____.

4.3 Total Ascent Times and Submerged Time on Decompression Dives

---

Example and Explanation

Total ascent time and submerged time on a ▼ 60'/61 dive are __3:00__ and __64:00__ , respectively.

The Standard Air Decompression Tables give both stop times and total ascent times for decompression dives. Total ascent times include stop times. Remember, ascent, stop, and submerged times read in minutes: seconds. ABT above is 61 minutes. Ascent time to the 10' stop is 0:50 (1'/second × 50'). Stop time at 10' is 2 minutes. Ascent time from the stop to the surface is 0:10 (1'/second × 10'). Total ascent time is 3:00 (0:50 + 2 minutes + 0:10). Submerged time is 64:00 (61 + 3:00).

Questions

A. The correct rate of ascent from the bottom to the deepest decompression stop, between decompression stops, and between the shallowest decompression stop and the surface, is _____ per minute. Total ascent time includes time spent swimming upward plus time at _____ _____, if any.

B. Begin timing decompression stops when you arrive at the correct _____, and resume your _____ when the specified time has elapsed. Time spent ascending to and between decompression stops is _____ included in decompression stop time.

Problems

1. Total ascent time and submerged time on a ▼ 60'/80 dive are _____ and _____ , respectively.

2. Total ascent time and submerged time on a ▼ 90'/35 dive are _____ and _____ , respectively.

3. Total ascent time and submerged time on a ▼ 100'/30 dive are _____ and _____ , respectively.

4. Total ascent time and submerged time on a C— ▼ 80'/30 dive are _____ and _____ , respectively.

5. Total ascent time and submerged time on a B— ▼ 100'/20 dive are _____ and _____ , respectively.

4.4 Omitted Decompression   For Emergency Use Only

Example and Explanation

On a ▼60'/65 dive, you accidentally ascend directly to the surface without making a decompression stop. The omitted decompression procedure requires the following stops: [_40'/0 : 30_] , [_30'/0 : 40_] , [_20'/1_] , [_10'/3_] .

   A ▼ 60/65 dive requires a [10'/2] stop. The procedure requires a 40' stop for ¼ the 10' stop time; a 30' stop for ⅓ the 10' stop time, a 20' stop for ½ the 10' stop time, and a 10' stop for 1½ times the scheduled 10' stop time. Remember, fractional stop times are shown in minutes:seconds.

Questions

A. If you do not make a necessary decompression stop, the U.S. Navy's omitted decompression procedure calls for an immediate return to the water, and specifies that you should repeat any required stops deeper than _____ ; stop at 40' for _____ of the scheduled 10' stop time; stop at 30' for _____ of the scheduled 10' stop time; stop at 20' for _____ of the scheduled 10' stop time; and stop at 10' for _____ times the scheduled 10' stop time.

B. The in-water omitted decompression procedure should only be used when no symptoms of _____ _____ are present; a recompression chamber is _____ _____ ; when good communication with the diver can be maintained; and when a _____ diver is available.

C. The omitted decompression procedure requires an ascent rate of _____ minute between stops, unlike the usual rate of ascent (_____ per minute) for other decompression and no-decompression procedures.

Problems

1. After a ▼ 70'/60 dive on which no decompression stops were made, the omitted decompression procedure calls for the following stops:

_____ .

2. After a ▼ 120'/16 dive on which no decompression stops were made, the omitted decompression procedure calls for the following stops:

_____ .

3. After a ▼ 80'/41 dive on which no decompression stops were made, the omitted decompression procedure calls for the following stops:

_____ .

4. After a B— ▼ 92'/35 dive on which no decompression stops were made, the omitted decompression procedure calls for the following stops:

_____ .

5. After a D— ▼ 75/30 dive on which no decompression stops were made, the omitted decompression procedure calls for the following stops:

_____ .

4.5 Fast Ascents

Examples and Explanations

At the end of a ▼ 100'/20 dive, you start an ascent. Only 0:40 has elapsed by the time you reach 10'. Your stop is [_10'40/1:40_] before surfacing.

Since the correct ascent rate would have gotten you to 10' in 1:30, (100' − 10' = 90', and 90' × 1'/second = 1:30) you're 0:50 early. You must stop at 10' for the 60'/minute ascent time from 100' to the surface. 100' × 1'/second = 1:40.

At the end of a ▼ 70'/60 dive, you start an ascent. Only 0:20 has elapsed by the time you reach 10'. Your stops are [_20'/0:40_] and [_10'/8_] before surfacing.

Since the correct ascent rate would have gotten you to 10' in 1:00 (70' − 10' = 60' and 60' × 1'/second = 1:00), you're 0:40 early. Your planned decompression stop is [_10'/8_]. You must now return to 20', make a [_20'/ 0:40_] stop and then make your 10' stop.

Note: Neither the U.S. Navy nor the NOAA Diving manuals cover fast ascents early in no-decompression dives, when you are not near the no-decompression limit. In this case, it would certainly do no harm to follow the procedure in the first example, and stop at 10' for the time the ascent would have taken at the normal rate.

Questions

A. If your ascent on a no-decompression dive is faster than normal and your TBT is within 10 minutes of the no-decompression limit, you should stop at _____ for the amount of time it would have taken to ascend to the surface at the normal rate.

B. If your ascent is faster than normal and if your dive requires a decompression stop, you should stop 10' _____ the first scheduled _____ _____ for the remaining time it would have taken to get to that stop if you had ascended at the normal rate.

Problems

1. At the end of a ▼ 60'/50 dive, you start an ascent. Only 0:40 elapses by the time you reach 10'. Your stop is _____.

2. At the end of an ▼ 80'/30 dive, you start an ascent. Only 0:50 elapses by the time you reach 10'. Your stop is _____.

3. At the end of a ▼ 92'/20 dive, you start an ascent. Only 0:50 elapses by the time you reach 10'. Your stop is _____.

4. At the end of an ▼ 80'/50 dive, you start an ascent. Only 0:30 elapses by the time you reach 10'. Your stop(s) is/are _____.

5. At the end of a ▼ 90'/31 dive, you start an ascent. Only 0:20 elapses by the time you reach 10'. Your stop(s) is/are _____.

4.6 Slow or Delayed Ascents

Examples and Explanations

After a ▼ 100'/25 dive, you begin an ascent but stop at 80' for 2 minutes. You then resume your ascent at the normal rate. Your revised ABT is _27min._, you should make a decompression stop of [_10'/3_], and you are then in group _I_.

The 1-minute delay occurred deeper than 50' so ABT is increased by 1 minute. The dive was already at the no-decompression limit, so the new ABT requires a [10'/3] stop, and puts you in group I instead of H.

At the end of a ▼ 70'/60 dive, you begin an ascent at the normal rate but slow down above 40', and find that 2:00 has elapsed by the time you reach 10'. Your stop is [_10'/9_].

You should have reached 10' in 1:00 but instead it takes 2:00. The delay occurred above 50', so the stop time is increased by 1 minute.

Questions

A. A delay in ascent may change your group at the end of the dive, or even force you to make _____ _____ when none would otherwise be required, or change your decompression schedule.

B. If your ascent on either a no-decompression or decompression dive is delayed at a depth greater than 50', you should consider your ABT to have been _____ by the _____ between actual ascent time and the time it would have taken to make the ascent at the normal rate.

C. If your ascent on a decompression dive is delayed at a depth shallower than 50', you should increase the _____ of the deepest decompression stop by the _____ between actual ascent time to that stop and the time it would have taken at the normal rate.

Note: The U.S. Navy Diving Manual does not specifically cover delays in ascent occurring at depths less than 50' on no-decompression dives. A safe procedure would be to increase ABT by the amount of the delay (as per delays deeper than 50'), and stop if indicated by the new ABT. Use this procedure for any applicable problems below.

Problems

1. At the end of a ▼ 100'/20 dive, you begin a normal ascent but stop at 60' for 2 minutes. You then resume your ascent at the normal rate. Your ABT is _____ , and you are in group _____.

2. At the end of a ▼ 90'/30 dive, you begin a normal ascent but stop at 70' for 1 minute. You then resume your ascent at the normal rate. Your ABT is _____ , your stop is _____ , and you are in group _____.

3. At the end of a ▼ 90'/40 dive, you begin a normal ascent but stop at 60' for 2 minutes. You then resume your ascent at the normal rate. Your ABT is _____ , your stop is _____ , and you are in group _____.

4. At the end of a ▼ 72'/30 dive, you begin a normal ascent but stop at 30' for 1

minute. You then resume your ascent at the normal rate. Your ABT is
_____ , and your are in group _____ .

5. At the end of a ▼ 110'/40 dive, you begin a normal ascent but stop at 45' for
2 minutes. You then resume your ascent at the normal rate. Your ABT is
_____ , your stop(s) is/are _____ , and you
are in group _____ .

4.7 Cold or Strenuous Dives

Example and Explanation

On a ▼ 90'/26 dive, you were exceptionally cold. You should consider the
dive equivalent to a ▼ _90'/40_ dive; your decompression stop should be
[_10'/7_], and you are in group _J_ .

For any dive during which you are very cold, or which is relatively
strenuous, the U.S. Navy procedure is to consider your bottom time equivalent to the next longer tabled time that which would normally pertain to
your dive, and use the repetitive group (and the decompression stop, if any)
appropriate for the longer time. A ▼ 90'/26 dive would normally put you in
group H. Since it was an exceptionally cold dive, you use the ▼ 90'/40
schedule (rather than ▼ 90'/30), make a [10'/7] stop, and are in group J at
the end of the dive.

Note: Standard practice for many commercial and research divers is to
use the next longer *and* next deeper schedule than those which would
normally pertain to your dive, if the dive is both cold *and* arduous. For
example, a ▼ 90'/26 hard-working dive in cold water would be considered
equivalent to a ▼ 100'/40 dive, requiring a [10'/15] stop, and putting you in
group K. Use this procedure for any problem involving both factors.

Problems

1. On a ▼ 60'/50 dive, you are exceptionally cold. You should consider the dive
equivalent to a _____ dive; your decompression stop(s) (if any) should
be _____ and you are in group _____ .

2. On an ▼ 80'/36 dive, you are exceptionally cold. You should consider the
dive equivalent to a _____ dive; your decompression stop(s) (if any)
should be _____ and you are in group _____ .

3. On a ▼ 100'/21 dive, you are exceptionally fatigued. You should consider the dive equivalent to a _____ dive; your decompression stop(s) (if any) should be _____ and you are in group _____.

4. On an ▼ 82'/30 dive, you are exceptionally cold and fatigued. You should consider the dive equivalent to a _____ dive; your decompression stop(s) (if any) should be _____ and you are in group _____.

5. On a ▼ 70'/50 dive; you are exceptionally cold and fatigued. You should consider the dive equivalent to a _____ dive; your decompression stop(s) (if any) should be _____ and you are in group _____.

4.8 High Altitudes After Diving

Examples and Explanations

After a ▼ 100'/25 dive, a surface interval of __2:24__ is required before leaving sea level, and you should not then fly in any aircraft above an altitude of __8,000__ ', or which cannot maintain a cabin pressure that does not exceed an equivalent altitude of __8,000__ '.

This is a no-decompression dive, after which you are in group H. You must be in group D to leave sea level. To get from group H to group D requires a minimum surface interval of 2:24. Even as a group D diver, you may not exceed 8,000' altitude.

After a single ▼ 100'/30 dive ending at 8:30 a.m., you may not fly in an airplane until at least __8:30 p.m.__.

This is a decompression dive, and you must not leave sea level until a surface interval of at least 12 hours after the dive.

Note: Most commercial aircraft maintain cabin pressure at the equivalent of about 8,000', or 0.74 atmosphere. The U.S. Navy Diving Manual specifies the minimum surface interval for flying in such aircraft after decompression dives (second example). It is vague on minimum surface interval for flying after no-decompression dives, but seems to specify 2 hours. The procedure in the first example is recommended by the National Oceanic and Atmospheric Administration (NOAA), and by most sport diving certification agencies. There is a growing trend to lengthen the minimum surface interval before flying after no-decompression dives to 12 hours, and after decompression dives to 24 hours. For the problems, use the procedures in the two examples.

Questions

A. After any no-decompression dive, you should be in group _____ or lower before flying or otherwise leaving sea level, and then not go to any higher altitude than _____ or the equivalent atmosphere pressure.

B. After any decompression dive, you should wait at least _____ hours before leaving sea level.

Problems

1. After a single ▼ 80'/39 dive, you should wait at least _____ before leaving sea level to fly in a commercial airliner.

2. After a D — ▼ 90'/14 dive, you should wait at least _____ before leaving sea level to drive into the mountains, and you should not go any higer than an altitude of _____.

3. After a C — ▼ 60'/40 dive, you should wait at least _____ before leaving sea level to fly in a light plane at an altitude of 8,000'.

4. After a single ▼ 65'/55 dive ending at 3:30 p.m., you should wait until at least _____ before leaving sea level to fly in a commercial airliner.

5. After a J — ▼ 50'/20 dive ending at 11 a.m., you should until wait at least _____ before leaving sea level to fly in a commercial airliner.

COMMENTS

In this section, we've covered some procedures that are typically very poorly understood by sport divers. You now know how to determine if decompression stops are required on any dive, and can find out how deep and long those stops should be. You've also learned the omitted decompression procedure for making up missed decompression stops. You have wrestled with the somewhat complex rules for fast and slow ascents. The faster-than-normal ascent procedure for no-decompression dives is easy to remember: if you're within 10 minutes of the no-decompression limit or ABT_{max}, just stop at 10' for the amount of time that the complete ascent would have taken at the correct rate. In other words, 1 second per foot of depth. For example, if you have just completed a 90′ dive and made a fast ascent, stop at 10′ for 90 seconds. The slower-than-normal ascent procedure for no-decompression dives is easy to remember, too: increase your ABT by the amount of the delay, and then make any stops that might be required by the revised ABT.

By the way, the use of submerged time (rather than bottom time) on no-decompression dives sidesteps all of the difficulties of correcting for slower-than-normal ascents. Using submerged time should get you back to the surface at the same time that your no-decompression bottom time runs out. If you had been operating on bottom time, you would then be beginning an ascent, with the potential for a delay en route. Using submerged time, you're already through with the dive and thus in no danger of exceeding the no-decompression limit or ABT_{max}.

You are also familiar with the special procedures for exceptionally cold or strenuous dives. If the dive is very cold or very fatiguing, consider your bottom time to have been the next longer tabled time than that which would normally apply. If the dive is both cold and hard, consider the dive to have been to the next greater depth and the next longer tabled time than those which would normally apply.

Finally, you've learned that you can't just hop on the plane at the end of a long dive trip. You must have a minimum surface interval at sea level before leaving going to higher altitudes after diving. That interval depends on the profile of your last dive, and whether or not it was a no-decompression dive.

Now that you've worked all of the questions and problems, you understand the U.S. Navy air decompression tables, and the correct procedures for using them. They will almost certainly be the standard for most sport divers for many years to come. From time to time, rumors of changes to the tables sweep the sport diving industry. You may have wondered whether or not these rumors are true, and whether or not you'll have to learn a new system. While revisions have been proposed by various authorities (though not by the U.S. Navy), most of them just recommend reduced no-decompression limits, and/or a decompression stop for safety's sake. The basic procedures for working the alternative tables generally don't differ from those you have just learned. For more on the subject of safety, we recommend that you reread pages 11–13, "A Word to the Wise."

APPENDIX: An Explanation of the Differences Between Decompression Table Procedures for Shallow Dives (35' or Less)

For a first dive to any depth (shallow dives included), you have already learned that you find out your group at the end of the dive using the first table (No-decompression Limits and Repetitive Group Designation Table for No-decompression Air Dives). For example, it's easy to see that you would be in group D after 100 minutes at 20'. For repetitive dives to shallow depths, though, there is currently some debate as to what group and what RNT you should use at the beginning of the dive.

The RNT you must account for at the beginning of a repetitive shallow dive is unlikely to limit your ABT since the no-decompression limits are many hours. However, the group at the start of any dive does directly affect the TBT at the end of the dive. This is important if you need to make a deeper repetitive dive later. There are two methods currently in use for determining RNT for dives shallower than 40'.

The original U.S. Navy procedure considers repetitive dives shallower than 40' as if they were 40' dives. You find your RNT and ABT_{max} for the group you are in at the beginning of the dive, using the 40' schedule. At the end of the dive, figure your TBT. This TBT is then used on the first table as if it were spent at 40' to determine your group. This method is more conservative than Method 2, as it assigns higher groups at the end of shallow dives. For example, a group F diver begins a 25' dive. He has 61 minutes RNT and an ABT_{max} of 139 minutes. He spends 35 minutes ABT. His TBT is thus 96 minutes and he is then in group I.

A second method has been developed recently. The method is less conservative than Method 1, as it assigns you lower groups at the end of shallow dives. It's a bit harder to describe, but it's easy to do. In fact, many tables have done it for you, supplying groups and RNT for the entire depth range. The rationale for the method is similar to that used for the exception rule. Let's assume, for example, that you make a single 25' dive for 125 minutes. At the end of the dive, you are in group F. Now, let's come at the situation from a different angle. What if you were already in group F from a previous dive, and were beginning a repetitive dive to 25'? Perhaps you might consider the two cases equivalent, ignoring the actual dive profile that got you into group F and just assuming that a group F diver is a group F diver, no matter how you got there.

If so, theoretically you can use an RNT of 125 minutes for the repetitive dive to 25'. You then add your ABT at 25' to the 125 minute RNT and arrive at a TBT at 25', rather than going to the 40' schedule. Finally, you look up your group on the 25' schedule. For example, a group F diver begins a 25' dive. He has 125 minutes RNT and he spends 35 minutes ABT. His TBT is 160 minutes, and he is then in group G.

Some sets of tables use Method 2 and have printed RNT and ABT_{max} for 35' dives (the shallowest dive having a no-decompression limit), and RNT for dives from 10'–30'. To use these tables for shallow dives, you determine your group in the same way you would for any depth. Other tables stick to the traditional method and don't print RNT or ABT_{max} for dives shallower than 40'. Can you use both methods on Problem Set 2.10?

If you want to astound your friends (and your diving instructor), you can use either method with any set of tables. You can determine RNT for shallow repetitive dives using Method 2 even if your tables list only RNT or ABT_{max} for dives to 40' and deeper. On the other hand, you can use Method 1 on any set of tables. It sounds tough, but it's easy. Here's how:

If you take a careful look at Method 2 tables, you'll find that RNT for dives in the 10'–35' depth range are identical to the maximum times listed for each group in the No-Decompression Limits and Repetitive Group Designation Table, for any given depth. For example, if you make a single dive to 30' for 45 minutes, you'll be in group C. If you began a repetitive dive as a group C diver, you'll find that Method 2 tables list 45 minutes as the RNT for 30'. If you were a group C diver and wanted to use Method 1 on any table for a repetitive dive to 30', you could look up the maximum single dive time at 40' that would put you in group C. You'd find 25 minutes, and add it to your ABT to get a TBT, and then determine your repetitive group for 40'.

By comparison, if you were a group C diver and wanted to use Method 2 on a set of tables that didn't list RNT for shallow dives, you would first look up the maximum single dive bottom time at 25' that would put you in group C (55 minutes). You would use this as your RNT, add it to your ABT to get TBT, and then determine your group as if it were an equivalent single dive at 25'.

ANSWERS

SECTION 1

1.1 **A.** surface, descent, bottom, ascent
  B. maximum, bottom time
  C. directly, decompression stops
  D. depth
  E. no-decompression limit
  F. 35′

  1. not defined
  2. 200 minutes
  3. 60 minutes
  4. 30 minutes
  5. 15 minutes

1.2 **A.** maximum, chest
  B. maximum

  1. 25, 100′, 25 minutes
  2. 43, 60′, 60 minutes
  3. 50, 70′, 50 minutes
  4. 20, 110′, 20 minutes
  5. 25, 100′, 25 minutes

1.3 **A.** bottom, ascent
  B. 60′
  C. less, ascending

  1. 31:00, 1:00
  2. 31:30, 1:30
  3. 12:00, 2:00
  4. 22:00, 2:00
  5. 73:30, 0:30

1.4 **A.** listed
  B. greater

  1. 100 minutes
  2. 100 minutes
  3. 50 minutes
  4. 30 minutes
  5. 60 minutes

SECTION 2

2.1 **A.** nitrogen
  B. bottom time
  C. greater
  D. deep

  1. D
  2. F
  3. F
  4. H
  5. C

2.2 **A.** listed
  B. greater
  C. longer

  1. F
  2. G
  3. H
  4. I
  5. H

2.3 **A.** surfacing, descent
  B. group
  C. exceed

  1. 1:40, 2:50
  2. 1:30, 3:58
  3. 2:59, 4:26
  4. D, C
  5. L, L

2.4 **A.** 0:10, previous, greatest
  B. 12:00

  1. 30 minutes
  2. 15 minutes
  3. 5:49, 12:01
  4. 2:11
  5. 12:01

2.5 **A.** repetitive

58

B. group, depth
C. lower

1. 47 minutes
2. 24 minutes
3. 24 minutes
4. 11 minutes
5. 10 minutes

2.6 **A.** any
B. total bottom
C. residual nitrogen, actual

1. 24 minutes, 31 minutes, 55 minutes, I
2. 20 minutes, 8 minutes, 28 minutes, H
3. 5 minutes, 31 minutes, 36 minutes, G
4. 26 minutes, 19 minutes, 45 minutes, I
5. 43 minutes, 5 minutes, 48 minutes, J

2.7 **A.** maximum, residual nitrogen time, no-decompression limit
B. no-decompression limit

1. 53 minutes
2. 6 minutes
3. 36 minutes
4. 49 minutes
5. 11 minutes

2.8 **A.** less
B. no-decompression limits, depth

1. 50′
2. 40′
3. 50′
4. 110′
5. 80′

2.9 **A.** actual, residual nitrogen
B. same, greater

1. 20 minutes
2. 10 minutes
3. 8 minutes
4. 2 minutes
5. 13 minutes

2.10 **1.** 17 minutes, 77 minutes, H (Method 1); 35 minutes, 95 minutes, E (Method 2)
2. 37 minutes, 85 minutes, I (Method 1); 40 minutes, 88 minutes, H (Method 2)
3. 49 minutes, 124 minutes, K (Method 1); 135 minutes, 210 minutes, G (Method 2)
4. 25 minutes, 55 minutes, G (Method 1) 110 minutes, 140 minutes, D (Method 2)

5. 7 minutes, 56 minutes, G (Method 1) 60 minutes, 109 minutes, B (Method 2)

SECTION 3

3.1 **1.** 30, 22, 13
2. 40, 16, 44
3. 30, 13, 44
4. 50, 30, 24
5. 100, 79, 113

3.2 **1.** 100, L, C, 79, L, H, 113, N, J, 84, N
2. 50, J, G, 16, J, I, 24, L, L, dive 4 exceeds tabled limits
3. 25, H, D, 14, H, G, 13, J, J, 13, L
4. 15, F, C, 15, H, B, 32, I, F, 24, J
5. 100, L, B, 49, J, J, 13, L, E, H (Method 1) or F (Method 2)

3.3 **1.** F, 3:58, B, I, 0:10, I
2. I, 1:00, G, J, 1:20, G
3. J, 0:55, H, L, 3:37, D
4. H, 3:21, C, H, 8:00, A
5. D, 2:39, B, I, 5:13, B

3.4 **1.** 22, G, D, J, F, 50′
2. 20, G, D, J, H, 50′
3. 10, C, C, J, G, 60′
4. 25, F, E, L, G, 40′
5. 35, G, E, J, J, 50′

SECTION 4

4.1 **A.** directly, decompression stops
B. depth, chest, time
C. no-decompression limit
D. greater, longer

1. [10′/10], K
2. [10′/8], K
3. [10′/18], L
4. [10′/3], I
5. [10′/7], L

4.2 **A.** decompression stop, 10′
B. depths, time

1. [10′/3]
2. [20′/2], [10′/24]
3. [10′/10]
4. [10′/3]
5. [10′/5]

4.3 **A.** 60', decompression stop
    B. depth, ascent, not

    1. 8:00, 88:00
    2. 8:30, 43:30
    3. 4:40, 34:40
    4. 11:20, 41:20
    5. 4:40, 24:40

4.4 **A.** 40', ¼, ⅓, ½, 1½
    B. decompression sickness, not available, standby (safety)
    C. one, 60'

    1. [40'/2], [30'/2:40], [20'/4], [10'/12]
    2. [40'/0:30], [30'/0:40], [20'/1], [10'/3]
    3. [40'/2:30], [30'/3:20], [20'/5], [10'/15]
    4. [40'/6], [30'/8], [20'/12], [10'/36]
    5. [40'/2:30], [30'/3:20], [20'/5], [10'/15]

4.5 **A.** 10'
    B. below, decompression stop

    1. [10'/1]
    2. [10'/1:20]
    3. [10'/1:32]

    4. [20'/0:40], [10'/10]
    5. [20'/1], [10'/7]

4.6 **A.** decompression stops
    B. increased, difference
    C. time, difference

    1. 22 minutes, G
    2. 31 minutes, [10'/7], J
    3. 42 minutes, [10'/18], L
    4. 31 minutes, H
    5. 40 minutes, [20'/4], [10'/21], L

4.7 **1.** ▼ 60'/55, none, I
    2. ▼ 80'/50, [10'/10], K
    3. ▼ 100'/25, none, H
    4. ▼ 100'/40, [10'/15], K
    5. ▼ 80'/60, [10'/17], L

4.8 **A.** D, 8,000'
    B. 12

    1. 2:45
    2. 2:24, 8,000'
    3. 3:05
    4. 3:30 a.m.
    5. 11 p.m.

CALCULATIONS

CALCULATIONS

FREE   FREE   FREE

Now that you have worked all the problems in this book, you will want to protect it for future reference.

Send for your FREE WATERPROOF ENCLOSURE by completing the coupon below and sending it to:

Pisces Books
P.O. Box 678
Locust Valley, NY 11560

Pisces Books
P.O. Box 678
Locust Valley, NY 11560

Please send me my free waterproof enclosure.

I have been diving for _____ years.

I make about _____ out-of-state dive trips per year.

Name _____

Address _____

City _____ State _____ Zip _____